SOUL *of* LIGHT

JOMA SIPE
SOUL *of* LIGHT
Works of Illumination

THEOSOPHICAL PUBLISHING HOUSE
Wheaton, Illinois ■ Chennai, India

QUEST BOOKS

    Theosophical Publishing House
    PO Box 270
    Wheaton, Illinois 60187-0270
    www.questbooks.net

The author thanks The Foundation for Inner Peace for permission to
reproduce quotations from *A Course in Miracles*.

Cover and book design and typesetting by Drew Stevens

Library of Congress Cataloging-in-Publication Data

Sipe, Joma.
Soul of light: works of illumination / Joma Sipe.
    p.   cm.
ISBN 978-0-8356-0904-3
1. Sipe, Joma, 1974—Themes, motives. I. Sipe, Joma, 1974—Works.
Selections 2012. II. Title.
ND833.S546 A4
759.69—dc23   2012007952

Printed in China

5 4 3 2 1 * 12 13 14 15 16

Contents

Foreword

From the unreal lead me to the Real.
        —Brihad-Aranyaka Upanishad 1.3.28

When I first saw Joma Sipe's paintings, the artist and his works were unknown to me. At first glance the geometric imagery seemed quite familiar, for I had seen and created similar forms as a designer, artist, and teacher of systems theory and sacred geometry. On second glance I noted an extraordinary quality in Joma's work, something I had not seen before: a vibrant, living light that seems to come from within. This quality resonated with me to the core of my being and stirred my curiosity to uncover what the work was really about.

Of course, even those less conditioned than I am to geometric imagery will likely be mesmerized by the visual power of the paintings in this volume: the craft and exactitude; the intricacy of lines and patterns; the complex interweaving of surfaces, colors, and textures; the clarity of form that also tricks the eyes— each providing an inescapable sense of intrigue and delight. Still others may be attracted by the metaphysical symbols, figurative or abstract, used in many of them. Perhaps the most striking feature is the use of crystals on many of these canvases. The astonishing

luminosity they create is perfectly suited to the visual structures, and so obvious is the energy emanating from them that one wonders why others never used this technique before! Yet, to stay with the works reveals there is much more to experience.

In this book Joma shares his story of these paintings. He describes his background of early study in esoteric subjects, how he was brought into the creative process to manifest his vision, and why he came to use these particular forms, structures, spaces, and devices. We learn much about the depth of his own perceptions that inspired his capacities to create this singular body of work.

For me, this process has an interesting parallel with what modernists experienced a century ago that produced the abstract art with which we are familiar today. Not surprisingly, these artists were profoundly stimulated by the growing interest in the metaphysical, especially guided by theosophy as the perennial wisdom that renders life and the purpose of art more intelligible. Artists like Piet Mondrian and Wassily Kandinsky come to mind, both heavily influenced by theosophy. Mondrian was an instrumental participant in the Dutch *De Stijl* (The Style) movement founded in 1917. Inspired by utopian ideals, its members sought to produce art that went beyond the figurative tradition in order to capture the spiritual in art. Theo van Doesburg, the intellectual leader of the group who especially propagated its ideals, in 1930 formed another group and art movement called Concretism, which was, as he stated, "a name I created since for us the so-called abstract spiritual is completely Concrete." In other words, the search was for the spiritual essence in the work, the noumenal Reality (or Truth) within versus the ordinary or phenomenal reality of appearances. After coining his term *concretism*, others like Kandinsky immediately declared themselves (as true students of theosophy) also "concretists" vs. abstractionists. Eventually, however, especially due to the influence of Max Bill, who interpreted Concretism as "art on the basis of mathematical thinking," Concretism evolved into genuine abstractionism with forms simply being intentionally free from any figurative and symbolic meaning.

I truly value van Doesburg's original reversal of the words *concrete* and *abstract* because for me it captures the aforementioned "utopian ideals" that were grounded in theosophy: a search for the Real within our ordinary (or "unreal") reality. When we apply that principle to the creative process, the resulting work of art mediates both realities, with visible form meant to stimulate the depth of perception into the Truth of (noumenal) Reality. To precipitate this relationship the artist must become fully engaged in a contemplative experience— which can only evolve from a complete state of attention wherein being and action are one. This process goes beyond what our minds can ordinarily comprehend, as a mysteriously, intuitive unfolding of that which is deep within ourselves.

Joma Sipe's work comes exactly from such deep contemplative practice. As he says in his preface, "Some of the drawings and figures are very strange to me, but somehow something inside of me understands all of it completely." His unique practice of adding crystals stems from the same practice, as we know from his statement: "At this stage, I must use all my sensibility, intuition, and inner vision in order to know which points to energize."

His gift here is to enable us to enter into his contemplative process with him through his paintings and poetry. My guess is that these works will resonate with the reader's very core of being as they do with mine—which is where the real power in this book lies.

—Thomas Ockerse
Professor of Graphic Design
Rhode Island School of Design
April 23, 2012

Preface

I was born in the city of Porto, Portugal, on August 2, 1974, and spent most of my childhood in the city of Vila Nova de Gaia, near Porto, where I still live and have my studio. At a very early age, perhaps seven or nine years old, I began painting; and I remember always drawing whatever appeared in my mind—not just the objects in front of me but also the ones that I could see in my imagination. At first my focus was on ordinary motifs such as landscapes and faces, using oils and acrylics with exuberant colors. Eventually, though, I realized that these subjects were not what I wanted to use to express my inner spiritual feelings, which was my goal almost from the outset.

At a very early age—about fifteen—I started feeling an restless urge to discover the reasons for living on this planet and to answer the ultimate questions: where do we come from, what are we doing here, and where are we going? These questions took me to the public library in Porto where I found old books in Portuguese by the early Theosophists Helena P. Blavatsky and Annie Besant. Having the opportunity to read Blavatsky's *Isis Unveiled*, *The Secret Doctrine*, and *The Voice of the Silence*, among other texts, I soon realized a profound and inexplicable deep connection with her and her teachings. Blavatsky's descriptions in *The Secret Doctrine* were not new to me; nor were the ideas of karma Besant describes so well in the lovely book entitled simply *Karma*. The ideas of the evolution and transmigration of the soul, as well as of the root races, the nature of the cosmos, the soul and its development, the septenary constitution of man, and the laws of reincarnation seemed totally familiar as I entered deeper and deeper into esoteric knowledge. One of Blavatsky's books that still influences my art today is *The Voice of the Silence*. All its words are highly inspired and can surely be used to enlighten the soul and raise the spirit.

Not knowing how to talk with others about these subjects, around the age of seventeen I saw an advertisement in the local newspaper for meditation and concentration courses. I went with avid curiosity to see what these courses were about and discovered that the ads had been placed by a mystical school called "The Gnostic Movement," created in 1950 by a Colombian who called himself Samael Aun Weor. To my delight, I found that the school was

Joma Sipe painting in his studio, with H. P. Blavatsky´s portrait as permanent inspiration.

spreading ideas I had already found in reading Blavatsky, Rudolf Steiner, Éliphas Lévi, G. I. Gurdjieff, and P. D. Ouspensky, among others. I studied there for some time, learning about the deeper esoteric aspects of various religions and philosophies, including the system of the chakras, occult anatomy, other dimensions, meditation and concentration techniques, depth psychology, alchemy, and the Kabbalah. I still have wonderful memories of the time spent among my friends discussing so many occult subjects at such an early age, while most of my other friends were leading a "normal" and entirely different life.

At about the age of twenty-eight, I entered another mystical school, this one being more oriented to ritual and practical magic. There, with the aid of a Portuguese teacher, I spent some time practicing the methods recollected by Franz Bardon in his book, *Initiation into Hermetics*.

At the beginning of 2004, when I was approaching thirty, one of my closest friends gave me a copy of Paramahansa Yogananda's *Autobiography of a Yogi*. I loved the book and felt with Yogananda almost the same connection that I had felt with Blavatsky. Everything he described touched me deeply—all the places, the encounters with notable persons, his philosophy of yoga, and his entire way of living and set of beliefs. That connection with Yogananda made me feel very close to Hindu culture, religion, and rituals; and in 2005 and 2007 I had the opportunity to visit the wonderful country of India. There I was fortunate to learn a great deal about sacred geometry and sacred magic in the Hindu temples of cities such as Shirdi, Hampi, Mumbai, Bangalore, and Delhi.

At the same time I was developing a relationship with Hindu culture, I began reading Eckhart Tolle's *The Power of Now*, a book that has made a huge transformation in my life and my entire way of thinking. In turn, Tolle led me to *A Course in Miracles*, published by the Foundation for Inner Peace. While reading it I received a lot of energy that inspired the series of paintings you will find in this book, together with texts from some of the 365 lessons in *A Course in Miracles*.

At this present time, I am writing my own poetry as inspiration for the paintings, as you will find here as well.

Since childhood I have also been influenced by the painters of the late nineteenth-century Symbolist Movement, notably Gustave Moreau, Fernand Khnopff, and Arnold Böcklin, among others. Other artists who have affected my work include Johfra Bosschart and Diana Vandenberg. I am always interested in pure esoterism and all art related to it, all my art being influenced by the mystical aspects of legends, myths, and spirituality related to the inner energy of every human being.

Throughout my career, I believe that my paintings clearly reflect theosophical objectives: They not only provide an image of the nucleus of the universal brotherhood of humanity, being easily understood by all without distinction, they also encourage the study of comparative religion and philosophy. In my paintings I search as well to explain in detailed sacred geometry the laws of nature and the powers latent in humankind. To conclude, I now quote Blavatsky on her own creative process because I identify with the same kind of process, which has to do with entering into a world of mists and shadows and expressing what I see in that world. In writing to her sister Vera on the manner of her writing, she says:

You may disbelieve me, but I tell you that in saying this I speak but the truth; I am solely occupied, not with writing Isis, *but with Isis herself. I live in a kind of permanent enchantment, a life of visions and sights, with open eyes, and no chance whatever to deceive my senses! I sit and watch the fair goddess constantly. And as she displays before me the secret meaning of her long lost secrets, and the veil becoming with every hour thinner and more transparent, gradually falls off before my eyes, I hold my breath and can hardly trust to my senses! . . . For several years, in order not to forget what I have learned elsewhere, I have been made to have permanently before my eyes all that I need to see.*

Thus, night and day, the images of the past are ever marshaled before my inner eye. Slowly, and gliding silently like images in an enchanted panorama, centuries after centuries appear before me . . . and I am made to connect these epochs with certain historical events, and I know there can be no mistake. Races and nations, countries and cities, emerge during some former century, then fade out and disappear during some other one, the precise date of which I am then told by . . . Hoary antiquity gives room to historical periods; myths are explained by real events and personages who have really existed; and every important, and often unimportant event, every revolution, a new leaf turned in the book of life of nations—with its incipient course and subsequent natural results—remains photographed in my mind as though impressed in indelible colors. . . .

When I think and watch my thoughts, they appear to me as though they were like those little bits of wood of various shapes and colours, in the game known as the casse-tête: I pick them up one by one, and try to make them fit each other, first taking one, then putting it aside until I find its match, and finally there always comes out in the end something geometrically correct. . . . I certainly refuse point-blank to attribute it to my own knowledge or memory, for I could never arrive alone at either such premises or conclusions. . . . I tell you seriously I am helped.

—H. P. Blavatsky, as quoted in Henry Steel Olcott, *Old Diary Leaves: The True Story of the Theosophical Society*, 1895

My sincere thanks to my friends all around the world who
have made this book possible. I wish to express my gratitude
to everyone at the Theosophical Society in America involved in
this project—especially Janet Kerschner, Sharron Dorr, and
Richard Smoley—and to my book designer, Drew Stevens.

Lokah Samastah Sukhino Bhavantu

May all beings in this universe be happy and free.
—HINDU ORAL TRADITION

Asato Maa Sas Gamaya
Tamaso Maa Jyotir Gamaya
Mrityor Maa Amritam Gamaya
Om Shanti Shanti Shanti

God, please lead me
From the unreal to the real,
From darkness to the light,
From death to immortality.
Om, peace, peace, peace.
—BRIHAD-ARANYAKA
UPANISHAD 1.3.28

The Painting Process

The intricate and elaborate process of creating each work includes the purpose of transmitting a message, although sometimes that message cannot be understood immediately. Each work disperses and concentrates the light that emanates from each line in the painting. This light represents Being and our deeper Essence, the deep heart of the energy from life that inhabits everything that exists. This energy seeks to break the barrier of the physical dimension to meld with the universal Energy that condenses, materializes, and takes form in each canvas.

My principal goal is to transmit, through the lines and crystals, an inner spiritual image or sacred feeling that I have. The various mystical schools, rituals, religions, and ways of thought I have studied—Theosophy, Gnosticism, the Kabbalah, Hinduism, and so on—only help me to process what I see inside and to transmit that vision to the paper or the canvas, using very simple materials and processes.

Usually I start with a blank canvas or piece of black paper without having any idea of what I am going to draw. I sit waiting for inspiration, and it surely comes within some minutes. As if

on their own, the very thin silver or gold ink pens start working until no more lines, circles, or other forms that make part of the work can be drawn. Some of the drawings and figures are very strange to me, but somehow something inside of me understands all it completely.

That completes the initial phase of creating a work of sacred geometry. The second phase has to do with locating the points in the painting to enhance with crystals. I use both simple crystals that do not reflect any color and shine only in a white, silver way as well as aurora boreal crystals that reflect every color that exists. At this stage, I must call on all my sensibility, intuition, and inner vision in order to know which points to energize. This process produces an energetic rebirth at the specific points of the painting, as new life is breathed inside the work that fills it with spiritual intensity. The crystals energize the painting and make the final adjustments to the proportion and balance that already exist in the sacred silver and gold lines that create the basic structure.

On some days I am inspired to use gold-ink pens exclusively and on others to use only silver-ink pens. Usually, though, my inspiration

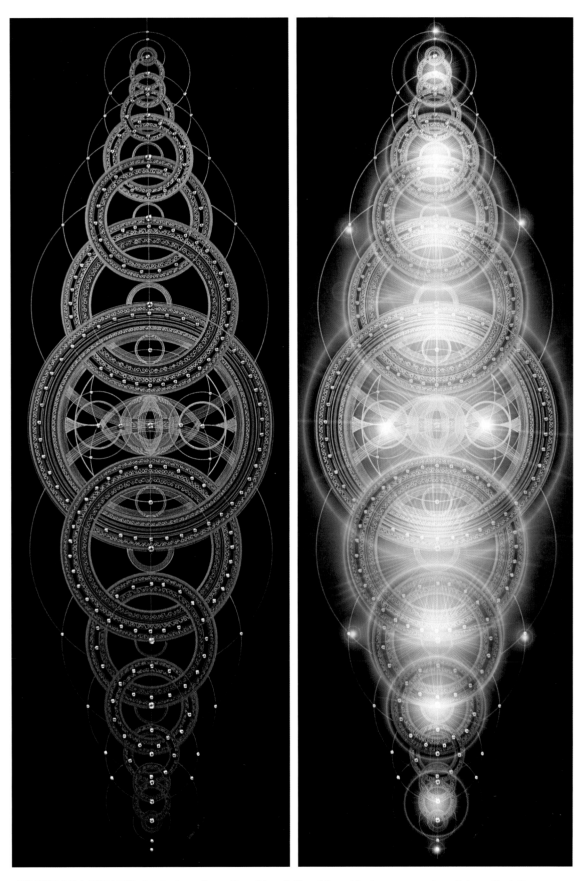

HOMOLOG 1 (TOUCH). *Original version with gold and silver ink on black canvas and crystals on the left; illuminated version on the right.*

leads me to draw with both and also to mix both crystal and aurora boreal crystals.

When I finish the black canvas or paper work with the gold or silver pens and crystals—which I call the "original work"—I start on the third phase of the process, or what I call the "illluminated work." At this stage I add light and soft-color computer effects, which give the paintings their ethereal quality. The lighting may vary from simple glowing drops to a radiance that infuses the entire piece.

These different effects and colors are chosen by the same process of inspiration through which I create the original paintings. Fortunately, this inspiration simply appears to me, so that I always know the exact effect and color to apply. Such elements add energy and luminosity to the original painting, reinforcing and completing the deeper connection between the work of art and what I see in my inner world.

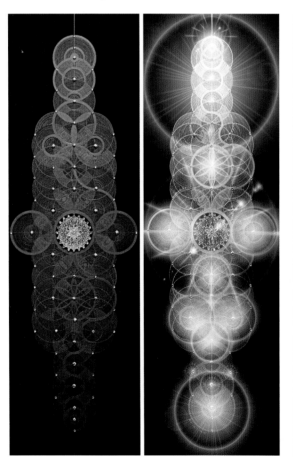

In the paintings on pages 14 and 15, the original version is on the left with the illuminated version on the right.

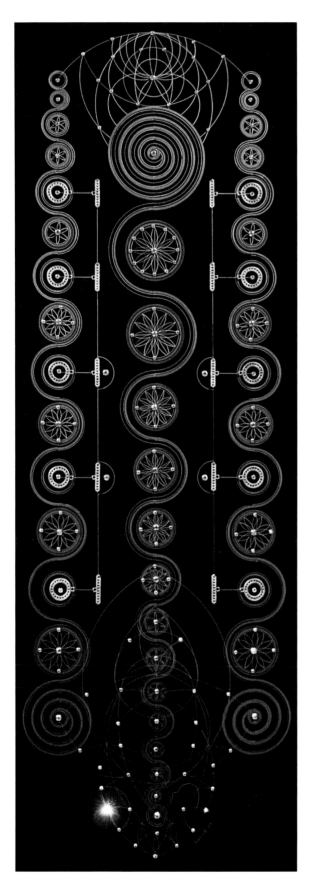 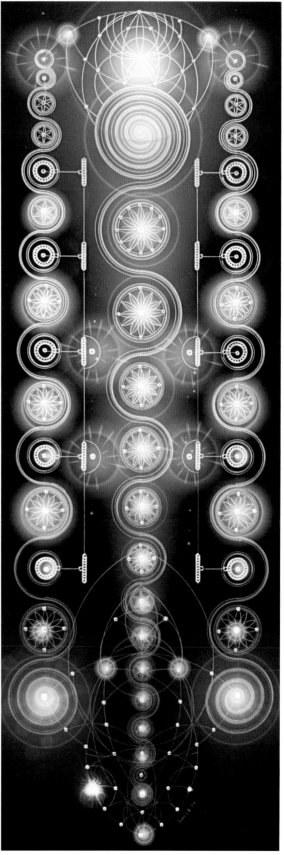

Chakras

I created this series of chakra paintings because I feel very interested in the internal light and energy system of the human form, which is connected with spiritual essence.

The word *chakra* in Sanskrit means "energy wheel" or "energy center." It is a term used in Hindu philosophy to designate the seven major energy centers in the human body, in which there is a deposit of creative energy that promotes balance. Hindus believe that obtaining a balance of these energy centers is the essential basis for the well-being in life of every human being.

The design I have chosen belongs to the Vedic philosophy of the chakras, together with the number of petals, which corresponds to the flourishing of the chakras and the awakening of the energy they contain. Each chakra is associated with a color, ranging from red for the root chakra at the base of the spine to violet for the crown chakra at the top of the head. In my work I incorporate these colors, which represent, for the clairvoyant, the essence of creative energy that resides in these centers of power condensed in the physical plane.

I have tried to create a geometric system based on the number of petals, the colors, and the original Sanskrit letters associated with the chakras to produce powerful mandalas. My hope is that these mandalas will allow the activation of each chakra in the energy body of each person who comes into contact with these paintings.

Also associated with this symbolism is the book of Revelation, or the Apocalypse, by John. I see in John's revelation of the Seven Churches a symbolic correspondence to the description of the seven chakra energy centers of the human body. In his 1928 book *The Secret Teachings of All Ages*, Manly P. Hall wrote that the Apocalypse corresponds to a treatise based on symbolism and the Kabbalistic system of numerology, the Tarot, and Vedic philosophy, all of which was well known to the early Gnostics, including the internal system of the Hindu chakras.

LICORNE AND CHAKRAS

Centers of light and power lie within your body.
It is your link with the universe:
The way you communicate with the world,
Extra physical, without dimension;
The form of knowing who you are
And what your appearance is
In the universes full of light.

(Panel in silver ink and crystals on black canvas,
60 x 200 cm, 2010)

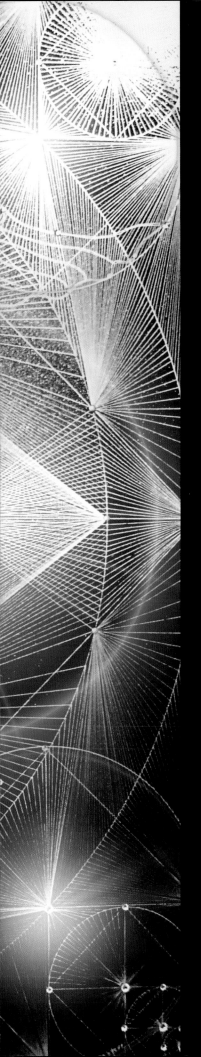

(Panel in gold and silver ink and crystals on black wood, 60 x 60 cm, 2006)

CHAKRA 1 (*MULADHARA—EPHESI ECCLESIÆ*)

When Light came to me I was the first born.
Inside your womb, Mother, I did not cry.
I did not ask for pleasure or any cloth to cover my body.
At first I had no shame and my entire body was perfect,
So perfect and balanced,
Knowing the way to go, as the river the sea recognizes.
I am now three times at sleep inside your womb, Mother.
I have honey in my lips and sweetness inside my heart.
I must awake, Mother,
And show myself to the entire, bitter world.
My blood is red and my veins taste like a calm breeze.

THE CHAKRAS   *(Panel in silver and gold ink and crystals
on black canvas, 90 x 90 cm, 2007)*

(Panel in gold and silver ink and crystals on black wood, 60 x 60 cm, 2006)

CHAKRA 2 (*SWADISTANA—SMYRNÆ ECCLESIÆ*)

I have awakened.

Doesn't my Soul sleep any more?

There are angel´s tears on the bed where I slept.

Starting now to climb the stairways to heaven,

I see the petals outside the flowers.

They appear orange to me.

They appear as open Light crossing a way flanked
    on both sides by sad trees.

I know now my pilgrimage Path.

The stars will always be at my feet.

Let the dark clouds disappear and the sun kiss my head.

I am the farewell in the last afternoon of a summer holiday.

These are the two sides of the rainbow.

(Panel in gold and silver ink and crystals on black wood, 60 x 60 cm, 2006)

CHAKRA 3 (*MANIPURA—PERGAMI ECCLESIÆ*)

The past exists no more.

I have reached the third level of knowledge inside.

There is no place for sadness, and tears find no rest here.

Yellow flowers blossom in my heart.

The fields are covered with green enchanted petals of yellow roses.

My body dresses with bright white light to receive love.

Come to me, gentle child.

Come to the arms of a Father that punishes no more,

Who loves and nothing asks in return.

I am One with the soul of the Father.

I am One with the Essence of the Mother.

(Panel in gold and silver ink and crystals on black wood, 60 x 60 cm, 2006)

CHAKRA 4 (*ANAHATA—THYATIRÆ ECCLESIÆ*)

Who knows?
Only the green open heart of the closed forests.
Who wants to know?
Only the perfect fool, looking for the Light Temple inside.
Keep looking, O fool of fools!
Keep longing for hope and with faith.
Never something so precious has ever been given to anyone: Faith.
With it you can move your own inner mountains.
Believe in your heart, dear child of God.
Inside of you lies the entire universe.
You are truly everything that exists.

(Panel in gold and silver ink and crystals on black wood, 60 x 60 cm, 2006)

CHAKRA 5 (*VISHUDDA — SARDIS ECCLESIÆ*)

Express the feelings.

Express yourself in blue waves of thought, care, and emotion.

Love the entire world until infinity.

As the wind blows softly above the seas,

Blow your love with kindly care through all your existence.

You can see now.

Everything can be seen by you.

Don't be afraid of the sunset.

Tomorrow there will always be a new sunrise,

A new blue dawn waiting for a way different from the one you chose

(Panel in gold and silver ink and crystals on black wood, 60 x 60 cm, 2006)

CHAKRA 6 (*AJNA—PHILADELPHIÆ ECCLESIÆ*)

You are almost there, little child.
Just let your imagination go free.
Set the fire in the candle of your heart.
Light your indigo veins with magic blood.
Let the third eye be open.
Let your intuition lead your footprints.
Let the sand on your path be softened by loving words.
You are almost there.
Heaven is near,
Just one cloud above.

(Panel in gold and silver ink and crystals on black wood, 60 x 60 cm, 2006)

CHAKRA 7 (*SAHASRARA—LAODICIÆ ECCLESIÆ*)

You have reached heaven,
Don't touch it; live inside it.
Don't think that is not for you; it is all that you are.
Don't think that you can't get there; it is already inside.
Just realize, little white child, the beauty of your crown.
All the angels sing now.
Together they praise the One who has reached the other side.
Only one shore, but so many ships that sail to it.
Only one sand, but so many footprints that go nowhere.
Only one God, but so many Essences spreading his Love

The *Antahkarana*

For me, the *Antahkarana* is the cord that connects the Higher Manas, or the divine part of man, to the personal Soul. It is, as Blavatsky states below, a medium of communication between the two. The cord is the connection between the negative and the positive pole in each human being and passes through many positions between the two extremes. The children represented in the following paintings are connected by this cord to their Higher Self.

Antahkarana (Sk.), or Antaskarana. The term has various meanings, which differ with every school of philosophy and sect. Thus Sankârachârya renders the word as understanding; *others, as the* internal instrument, the Soul, formed by the thinking principle and egoism; *whereas the Occultists explain it as the* path *or* bridge *between the Higher and the Lower Manas, the divine* Ego, *and the* personal Soul *of man. It serves as a medium of communication between the two, and conveys from the Lower to the Higher Ego all those personal impressions and thoughts of men which can, by their nature, be assimilated and stored by the undying Entity, and be thus made immortal with it, these being the only elements of the evanescent* Personality *that survive death and time. It thus stands to reason that only that which is noble, spiritual and divine in man can testify in Eternity to his having lived.*

—H. P. Blavatsky,
The Theosophical Glossary

RESURRECTION

You know that within you
A world of Light and Love
Abides.
You're an Immortal Being,
Dressed with an Immensity of
Stars
And on your forehead
Diamonds of white shining
Light.
You have forgotten your
Immortality.
Choose again.
Be reborn from the ashes.
Revive not only the body,
But also the soul of which it forms a part.
No more will you be the son of
Death.
Open the Light within you,
And keep alive the flame that lies within
Yourself.

(Panel in silver and gold pen and crystals on
black canvas, 60 x 130 cm, 2007)

THE RETURN TO INNOCENCE

When the Eyes of the Heart are opened,
The Eyes of the Soul come to life.
You create with the Power of Heavens:
It is within your Pure Lake of Wisdom;
It is deep in the Spirit that lies inside.
Return to It.
Seek It.
When time comes you will see,
It will be the Return to your Essence,
The Return to Innocence.

(Panel in silver and gold ink and crystals on
black canvas, 60 x 130 cm, 2007)

ORATIO (PRAYER)

Tomorrow will come within two seconds.
It is never the same:
The blood that flows through your veins,
The hair that grows on your head,
The petals that are being opened.
It is never the same:
The prayer to the Inner Altar,
The song from your lips,
The understanding of a child.

(Panel in silver and gold ink and crystals on black canvas, 60 x 130 cm, 2007)

UMBRA ALLARUM (THE SHADOW OF WINGS)

I now become one with the grass,
The wind,
And the flowers.
I arise inside by blessing the water
That falls from heaven.
Protect me in the Shadow of Your Wings.
Protect my voice,
My blood,
And my eyes,
So that I can seek only for the Truth.

(Panel in silver and gold ink and crystals on black canvas, 150 x 50 cm, 2007)

LACRYMOSA (TEARS FROM THE HEART)

Celestial Being. Winged Purity. Pure Virgin.
Chaste loved.
Lover Eternal. Of Lost Youth.
Never lasting dreams. Lost in life.
Steps of loneliness.
In your paths cross.
Laments wandering. Children of the winds.
Madness. Delights. Stray pride.
Broken mirrors. Empty of dreams.

*(Panel in silver and gold ink and crystals on
black canvas, 60 x 130 cm, 2007)*

Zodiacal, Magical, and Mystical Mandalas

These are a series of works that I made in a circular/quadrangular form known as "mandalas." *Mandala* is a Sanskrit word that means "circle." In the Hindu and Buddhist religious traditions, their sacred art often takes a mandala form. The basic form of most Hindu and Buddhist mandalas is a square with four gates containing a circle with a center point.

These mandalas, as concentric diagrams, have spiritual and ritual significance in both Buddhism and Hinduism. The term is of Hindu origin and appears in the Rig Veda.

In various spiritual traditions, mandalas may be employed for focusing attention of aspirants and adepts, as a spiritual teaching tool for establishing a sacred space, and as an aid to meditation and trance induction. In common usage, *mandala* has become a generic term for any plan, chart, or geometric pattern that represents the cosmos metaphysically.

These mandalas range from Leonardo da Vinci's drawing of the Vitruvian Man as a major symbol of the balanced proportions of the human body; to the Mayan calendar, the constellations, and the zodiacal symbols; and also as represented in magical, Hindu, and Kabbalistic art.

The "Flower of Life" design is also present in every geometric form that I want to act as a balance. It energizes every dark place or any mind in disorder.

Flower of Life Design

(Panel in silver and gold ink and crystals on black canvas, 90 x 90 cm, 2007)

MAN GOD

Days of eternity.
Sounds of Light and Silence.
Days of darkness

Know that the Light you seek
Is within you.
Know that immortality is yours.

(Panel in silver and gold ink and crystals on black canvas, 90 x 90 cm, 2007)

MAYA

I look at the sea, on this black day,
Gray obscured.
I ask you, Brother, to give me shelter
And calm my soul.
I was a storm and a free bird,
In the depths of the seas,
And now my eyes are submerged
And cannot settle down
With the movement of the wind.
And the sea is so stormy,
And my heart does not follow it.
Everything in me is at peace
And doesn't want more calm.
The waves that washed ashore
Remind me of you,
And I find another reason to cry.
This time I get lost
In the snowy white foam
That balances between
The pupils of my eyes.
And I dance the dance of the seagulls
On the top of the waves.

CONSTELLATIONS

Myriads of stars look for you.
The Divine takes care of you, and his eyes
always look for worship from you.
Whether you believe or do not believe it,
Whether you understand
Or do not understand,
There is a universe of Justice.
And the Eyes of Truth
Are always watching you.

(Panel in silver and gold ink and crystals on black canvas, 90 x 90 cm, 2007)

HEAVEN IN A WILD FLOWER

To see a world in a grain of sand,
And heaven in a wild flower,
Hold infinity in the palm of your hand,
And eternity in an hour.

■ ■ ■

HE WHO BINDS TO HIMSELF A JOY

He who binds to himself a joy
Does the winged life destroy;
He who kisses the joy as it flies
Lives in eternity's sunrise.

—William Blake

(Panel in silver and gold ink and crystals on black canvas, 90 x 90 cm, 2007)

NANGTEN MENLANG
(TIBETAN HEALING ART)

The way of life is only love,
Love is life.
If you have love you have all.
This is my gift for those who have
Hearts to understand these words.

—Tulku Lama Lobsang

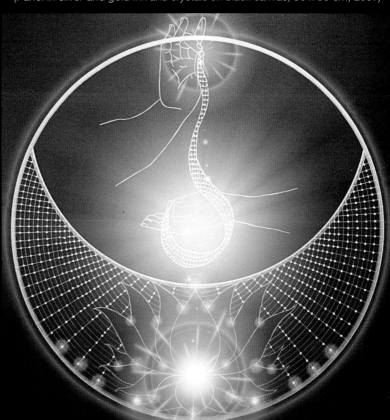

(Panel in silver and gold ink and crystals on black canvas, 90 x 90 cm, 2008)

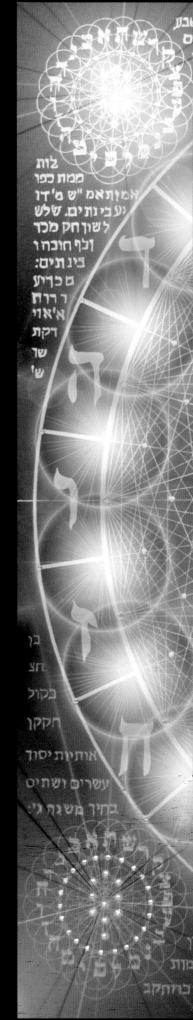

SEPHER YETZIRAH (BOOK OF CREATION)

They give me messages surrounded by circles of light.

Stone buildings resemble screaming heavens that claim for antiquity.

Within a circle of fire I protect me from myself,

Now that the rains have returned and the endless skies of gray are flooded.

My words belong to the sands,

And my lyrics are stars that are launched from infinite space.

The dead ones visit me, returning from the forgotten worlds,

And consume my blood.

I pray to the Heavens to forgive my mother for giving birth to me

And for the first time life was blown into me.

I pray to the Heavens to forgive my father for having his life in my life mixed

And for the last time death had breathed into me.

(Panel in silver and gold Ink and crystals on
black canvas, 90 x 90 cm, 2008)

(Panel in silver and gold ink and crystals on black canvas, 90 x 90 cm, 2009)

ESOTERIC PENTAGRAM

Head of a corpse, the Lord
Command thee by the living
And devoted serpent!
Cherub, the Lord command
Thee by Adam Yod-Havah!
Wandering eagle, the Lord
Command thee by the wings
Of the bull! Serpent,

The Lord Tetragrammaton
Command thee
By the angel and the lion!
Michael, Gabriel,
Raphael, and Anael!
Flow Moisture,
By the spirit of Elohim.
Earth, be established by

Adam Yod-Havah.
Let a firmament be created
By Yahveh Sabaoth.
Let judgment be created
By fire in the power of Michael.

—Éliphas Lévi, *The Dogma
and Ritual of High Magic*, 1855

(Panel in silver and gold ink and crystals on black canvas, 120 x 120 cm, 2008)

MY HEART BELONGS TO NO ONE

A thousand burning torches
Illuminate my darkness now,
And my heart burns and my pulse
Lives from your blood and light.
A thousand torches burn
Scaring away the loneliness.

A thousand torches burning giving
That to what already is.
Fire of fire and light of light.
Forgotten forever.
Lives go through my endless gaze
When I look at the pillars of light

Or the choices I made
And I left unfulfilled;
Promises of achievement and
Heights of burning opium.
Again on fire, I burn on the
Funeral pyre of your being.

(Panel in silver and gold ink and crystals on black canvas, 90 x 90 cm, 2008)

SIGILLUM DEI AMETH
(THE SEAL OF THE TRUTH OF GOD)

The magic and power are given to the Son
Who proceeds from the Father
And has all his attributes:
Power, Wisdom, Light, and Energy
That create constantly.

(Panel in silver and gold ink and crystals on black canvas, 90 x 90 cm, 2008)

SRI YANTRA

I am the petal inside the circle.
I am the flower inside the square.
I am the light inside the triangle.
I am the Petal.
I am the Flower.
I am Light.
I am the circle, the square, and the triangle.
Love is All that I Am.

THE WHEEL OF LIFE

In the Wheel of Life I have
Lost myself.
In the Wheel of Life I have
Found myself.
I have found in it the hugeness of the eyes
That look at me from
Childhood.
When the wheel circles without stop,
When it spins without stop,
It leads me to paths of
Tremendous ecstasies,
To paths of dawns that appear,
On the open hugeness
Of a space without end.

(Panel in silver and gold ink and crystals on black canvas, 70 x 70 cm, 2006)

THE ROAD OF THE SOUL

The night has come and with it
The hugeness of dreams
A long time forgotten
On the mist of the past
That comes after me.
The night has come and
No more white dawns
Obscure my eyes.
The dark shadows have fallen,
Covering with its dark cloth
My eyes and dreams.
And today I show myself to the world.
The night has come,
And with it the strength and courage
To make my inner Light shine.

(Panel in silver and gold ink and crystals on black canvas, 70 x 70 cm, 2006)

A Course in Miracles

I started reading the *Course* when I finished reading Eckhart Tolle's book *The Power of Now*, in which he mentions the *Course* two or three times. *A Course in Miracles* was originally written in a collaborative work between Helen Schucman and William Thetford.

In the beginning, the Voice (which Schucman claimed had identified itself earlier to her as Jesus Christ) described the two as "the scribes."

In 1975, *A Course in Miracles* was published and distributed as a three-volume set—which had evolved from the original notes—and comprised three books: text, a workbook for students, and a manual for teachers.

I become inspired while reading some passages of the book, and the images for the paintings started to flow slowly but very precisely. I knew all that I had to design as well as the passages that were to be chosen from the book.

Here is the first paragraph in the book, which describes the entire *Course*:

"This is a course in miracles. It is a required course. Only the time you take it is voluntary. Free will does not mean that you can establish the curriculum. It means only that you can elect what you want to take at a given time. The course does not aim at teaching the meaning of love, for that is beyond what can be taught. It does aim, however, at removing the blocks to the awareness of love's presence, which is your natural inheritance. The opposite of love is fear, but what is all-encompassing can have no opposite.

This course can therefore be summed up very simply in this way:
Nothing real can be threatened.
Nothing unreal exists.
Herein lies the peace of God."

—*A Course in Miracles*, Intro., p. 1

THE COMING OF THE HOLY SPIRIT
(Panel in silver and gold ink and crystals on black canvas, 90 x 70 cm, 2007)

THE DOOR OF HEAVEN *(Panel in silver and gold ink and crystals on black canvas, 90 x 70 cm, 2007)*.

THE VOICES OF SHADOWS *(Panel in silver and gold ink and crystals on black canvas, 90 x 70 cm, 2007)*

THE SYMBOLS OF LOVE *(Panel in silver and gold ink and crystals on black canvas, 90 x 70 cm, 2007)*

THE COMING OF THE HOLY SPIRIT

Around you angels hover lovingly, to keep away all darkened thoughts of sin, and keep the light where it has entered in. Your footprints lighten up the world, for where you walk forgiveness gladly goes with you.

—*A Course in Miracles*: T-26.IX.7:1–2

THE DOOR OF HEAVEN

Each day, and every minute in each day, and every instant that each minute holds, you but relive the single instant when the time of terror took the place of love. And so you die each day to live again, until you cross the gap between the past and present, which is not a gap at all. Such is each life; a seeming interval from birth to death and on to life again, a repetition of an instant gone by long ago that cannot be relived. And all of time is but the mad belief that what is over is still here and now.

Forgive the past and let it go, for it *is* gone. You stand no longer on the ground that lies between the worlds. You have gone on, and reached the world that lies at Heaven's gate. There is no hindrance to the Will of God, nor any need that you repeat again a journey that was over long ago. Look gently on each other, and behold the world in which perception of your hate has been transformed into a world of love.

—*A Course in Miracles*: T-26.V.13–14

THE VOICES OF SHADOWS

The Son whom God created is as free as God created him. He was reborn the instant that he chose to die instead of live. And will you not forgive him now, because he made an error in the past that God remembers not, and is not there? Now you are shifting back and forth between the past and present. Sometimes the past seems real, as if it *were* the present. Voices from the past are heard and then are doubted. You are like to one who still hallucinates, but lacks conviction in what he perceives. This is the borderland between the worlds, the bridge between the past and present. Here the shadow of the past remains, but still a present light is dimly recognized. Once it is seen, this light can never be forgotten. It must draw you from the past into the present, where you really are.

The shadow voices do not change the laws of time nor of eternity. They come from what is past and gone, and hinder not the true existence of the here and now. The real world is the second part of the hallucination time and death are real, and have existence which can be perceived. This terrible illusion was denied in but the time it took for God to give His Answer to illusion for all time and every circumstance. And then it was no more to be experienced as there.

—*A Course in Miracles*: T-26.V.11–12

THE SYMBOLS OF LOVE

The resurrection of the world awaits your healing and your happiness, that you may demonstrate the healing of the world. The holy instant will replace all sin if you but carry its effects with you. And no one will elect to suffer more. What better function could you serve than this? Be healed that you may heal, and suffer not the laws of sin to be applied to you. And truth will be revealed to you who chose to let love's symbols take the place of sin.

—*A Course in Miracles*: T-27.VI.8

*(Panel in silver and gold Ink and crystals on
black canvas, 90 x 70 cm, 2007)*

*(Panel in silver and gold ink and crystals on
black canvas, 90 x 70 cm, 2007)*

ANGELS HAVE COME

The holiest of all the spots on earth is where an ancient
hatred has become a present love. And They come quickly
to the living temple, where a home for Them has been set up.
There is no place in Heaven holier. And They have come to
dwell within the temple offered them, to be Their resting place
as well as yours. What hatred has released to love becomes
the brightest light in Heaven's radiance. And all the lights in
Heaven brighter grow, in gratitude for what has been restored.

Now is the temple of the Living God rebuilt as host again
to Him by Whom it was created. Where He dwells, His Son
dwells with Him, never separate. And They give thanks that
They are welcome made at last. Where stood a cross stands
now the risen Christ, and ancient scars are healed within His
sight. An ancient miracle has come to bless and to replace an
ancient enmity that came to kill. In gentle gratitude do God
the Father and the Son return to what is Theirs, and will forever be. Now is the Holy Spirit's purpose done. For They have
come! For They have come at last!

—*A Course in Miracles*: T-26.IX.6, 8

THE SOUNDS OF STILLNESS

How instantly the memory of God arises in the mind
that has no fear to keep the memory away. Its own
remembering has gone. There is no past to keep its
fearful image in the way of glad awakening to present
peace. The trumpets of eternity resound throughout the
stillness, yet disturb it not. And what is now remembered
is not fear, but rather is the Cause that fear was made to
render unremembered and undone. The stillness speaks
in gentle sounds of love the Son of God remembers
from before his own remembering came in between the
present and the past, to shut them out.

—*A Course in Miracles*: T-28.I.13

(Panel in silver and gold ink and crystals on black canvas, 90 x 70 cm, 2007)

(Panel in silver and gold ink and crystals on black canvas, 90 x 70 cm, 2008)

THE LADDER OF DREAM

This world is full of miracles. They stand in shining silence next to every dream of pain and suffering, of sin and guilt. They are the dream's alternative, the choice to be the dreamer, rather than deny the active role in making up the dream. They are the glad effects of taking back the consequence of sickness to its cause. The body is released because the mind acknowledges that "this is not done to me, but I am doing this." And thus the mind is free to make another choice instead. Beginning here, salvation will proceed to change the course of every step in the descent to separation, until all the steps have been retraced, the ladder gone, and all the dreaming of the world undone.

—*A Course in Miracles*: T-28.II.12

YOU WERE NOT BORN TO DIE

Change is the greatest gift God gave to all that you would make eternal, to ensure that only Heaven would not pass away. You were not born to die. You cannot change, because your function has been fixed by God. All other goals are set in time and change that time might be preserved, excepting one. Forgiveness does not aim at keeping time, but at its ending, when it has no use. Its purpose ended, it is gone. And where it once held seeming sway is now restored the function God established for His Son in full awareness. Time can set no end to its fulfillment, nor its changelessness. There is no death because the living share the function their Creator gave to them. Life's function cannot be to die. It must be life's extension, that it be as one forever and forever, without end.

—*A Course in Miracles*: T-29.VI.4

HEAVEN'S CALLING *(Panel in silver and gold ink and crystals on black canvas, 90 x 70 cm, 2008)*

ECHOES OF ETERNITY *(Panel in silver and gold ink and crystals on black canvas, 90 x 70 cm, 2008, private collection)*

THE THOUGHT OF GOD *(Panel in silver and gold ink and crystals on black canvas, 90 x 70 cm, 2008)*

GOD IS LOVE *(Panel in silver and gold ink and crystals on black canvas, 90 x 70 cm, 2008)*

NO LIGHT OF HEAVEN SHINES EXCEPT FOR YOU *(Panel in silver and gold ink and crystals on black canvas, 90 x 70 cm, 2007)*

HEAVEN'S CALLING

Yet all that happens when the gap is gone is peace eternal. Nothing more than that, and nothing less. Without the fear of God, what could induce you to abandon Him? What toys or trinkets in the gap could serve to hold you back an instant from His Love? Would you allow the body to say "no" to Heaven's calling, were you not afraid to find a loss of self in finding God? Yet can your Self be lost by being found?

—A Course in Miracles: T-29.I.9

ECHOES OF ETERNITY

There is a place in you where this whole world has been forgotten; where no memory of sin and of illusion lingers still. There is a place in you which time has left, and echoes of eternity are heard. There is a resting place so still no sound except a hymn to Heaven rises up to gladden God the Father and the Son. Where Both abide are They remembered, Both. And where They are is Heaven and is peace.

Think not that you can change Their dwelling place. For your identity abides in Them, and where They are, forever must you be.

—A Course in Miracles: T-29.V.1.2:1–2

THE THOUGHT OF GOD

Do you not understand that to oppose the Holy Spirit is to fight *yourself*? He tells you but *your* will; He speaks for *you*. In His Divinity is but your own. And all He knows is but your knowledge, saved for you that you may do your will through Him. God *asks* you do your will. He joins with *you*. He did not set His kingdom up alone. And Heaven itself but represents your will, where everything created is for you. No spark of life but was created with your glad consent, as you would have it be. And not one Thought that God has ever had but waited for your blessing to be born. God is no enemy to you. He asks no more than that He hear you call Him "Friend."

—A Course in Miracles: T-30.II.1

GOD IS LOVE

The fear of God results as surely from the lesson that His Son is guilty as God's love must be remembered when he learns his innocence. For hate must father fear, and look upon its father as itself. How wrong are you who fail to hear the call that echoes past each seeming call to death, that sings behind each murderous attack and pleads that love restore the dying world. You do not understand Who calls to you beyond each form of hate, each call to war. Yet you will recognize Him as you give Him answer in the language that He calls. He will appear when you have answered Him, and you will know in Him that God is Love.

—A Course in Miracles: T-31.I.10

NO LIGHT OF HEAVEN SHINES EXCEPT FOR YOU

Look once again upon your enemy, the one you chose to hate instead of love. For thus was hatred born into the world, and thus the rule of fear established there. Now hear God speak to you, through Him Who is His Voice and yours as well, reminding you that it is not your will to hate and be a prisoner to fear, a slave to death, a little creature with a little life.

Your will is boundless; it is not your will that it be bound.

What lies in you has joined with God Himself in all creation's birth. Remember Him Who has created you, and through your will created everything. Not one created thing but gives you thanks, for it is by your will that it was born.

No light of Heaven shines except for you, for it was set in Heaven by your will.

—A Course in Miracles:T-30.II.3

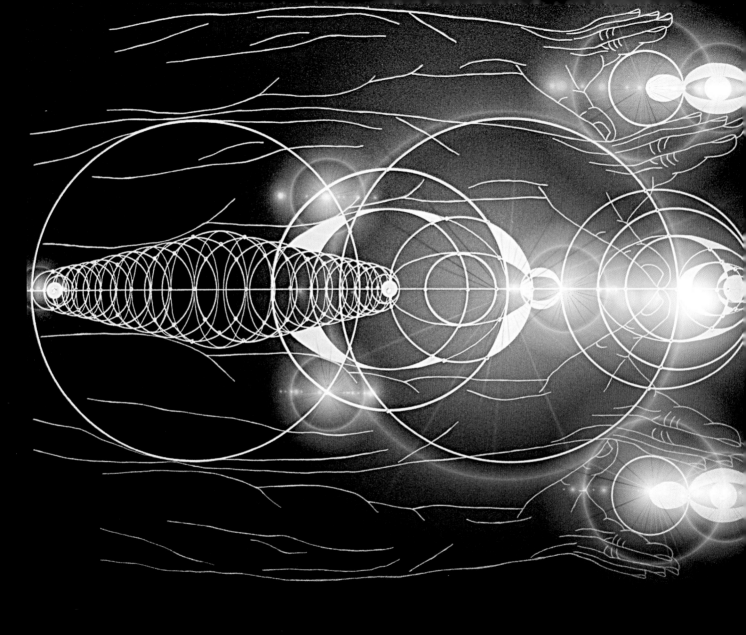

(Panel in silver and gold ink and crystals on black canvas, 2 x 90 x 70 cm, 2008)

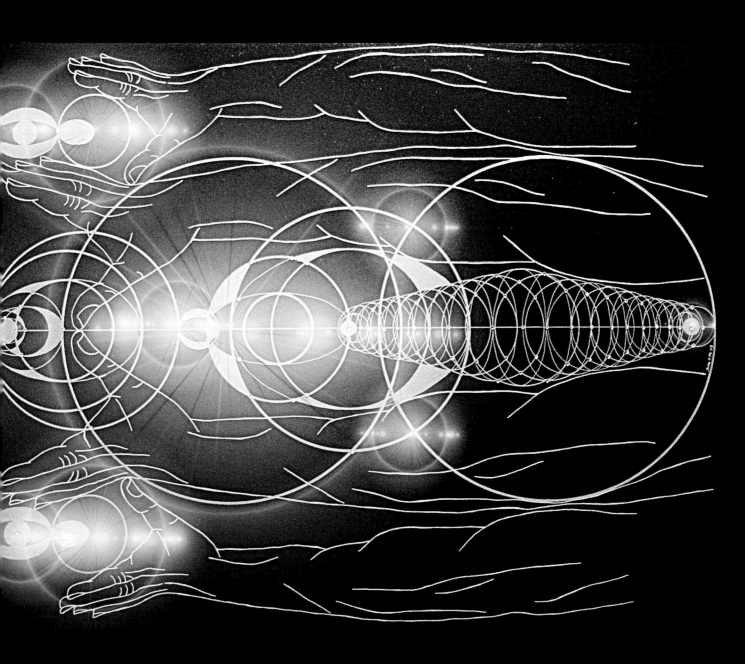

THERE IS NO WILL EXCEPT THE WILL OF LOVE

*How foolish, Father, to believe Your Son could cause himself
to suffer! Could he make a plan for his damnation, and be left
without a certain way to his release? You love me, Father. You
could never leave me desolate, to die within a world of pain and
cruelty. How could I think that Love has left Itself? There is no
will except the Will of Love. Fear is a dream, and has no will that
can conflict with Yours. Conflict is sleep, and peace awakening.
Death is illusion; life, eternal truth. There is no opposition to
Your Will. There is no conflict, for my will is Yours.*
　　　　　　　　　　　—*A Course in Miracles*: W-pII.331.1

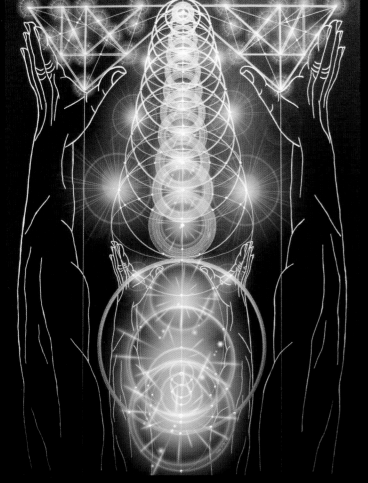

(Panel in silver and gold ink and crystals on
black canvas, 90 x 70 cm, 2008)

(Panel in silver and gold ink and crystals on
black canvas, 90 x 70 cm, 2008)

I AM FOREVER AN EFFECT OF GOD

*Father, I was created in Your Mind, a holy Thought that never left
its home. I am forever Your Effect, and You forever and forever
are my Cause. As You created me I have remained. Where You
established me I still abide. And all Your attributes abide in
me, because it is Your Will to have a Son so like his Cause that
Cause and Its Effect are indistinguishable. Let me know that
I am an Effect of God, and so I have the power to create like
You. And as it is in Heaven, so on earth. Your plan I follow here,
and at the end I know that You will gather Your effects into the
tranquil Heaven of Your Love, where earth will vanish, and all
separate thoughts unite in glory as the Son of God.*

LOVE´S REFLEX

*Our Father, bless our eyes today. We are Your messen-
gers, and we would look upon the glorious reflection of
Your Love which shines in everything. We live and move
in You alone. We are not separate from Your eternal life.
There is no death, for death is not Your Will. And we abide
where You have placed us, in the life we share with You
and with all living things, to be like You and part of You
forever. We accept Your Thoughts as ours, and our will is
one with Yours eternally.*

—*A Course in Miracles*: W-pl.163.9

(Panel in silver and gold ink and crystals on black canvas, 90 x 70 cm, 2007)

TODAY I DON´T WANT TO DREAM

If I accept that I am prisoner within a body, in a world in which all things that seem to live appear to die, then is my Father prisoner with me. And this do I believe, when I maintain the laws the world obeys must I obey; the frailties and the sins which I perceive are real, and cannot be escaped. If I am bound in any way, I do not know my Father nor my Self. And I am lost to all reality. For truth is free, and what is bound is not a part of truth.

Father, I ask for nothing but the truth. I have had many foolish thoughts about myself and my creation, and have brought a dream of fear into my mind. Today, I would not dream. I choose the way to You instead of madness and instead of fear. For truth is safe, and only love is sure.

Meditations with the Tree of Life

These are four series of works that I have done with a version from a drawing by Johfra Bosschart and the using of the Tree of Life. They are meant for inspiration and meditation. The Tree of Life is formed by ten spheres (called the Sephirot) and twenty-two branches, which are meant to be the twenty-two letters of the Hebraic alphabet. The composition as shown is full of vibrant energetic light, and the form of which it is disposed can be intended to induce meditate states and balance any internal disorder inside the human form.

Trees of Life: From the highest antiquity trees were connected with the gods and mystical forces in nature. Every nation had its sacred tree, with its peculiar characteristics and attributes based on natural, and also occasionally on occult properties, as expounded in the esoteric teachings. Thus the peepul or Âshvattha of India, the abode of Pitris (elementals in fact) of a lower order, became the Bo-tree or ficus religiosa of the Buddhists the world over, since Gautama Buddha reached the highest knowledge and Nirvâna under such a tree. The ash tree, Yggdrasil, is the world-tree of the Norsemen or Scandinavians. The banyan tree is the symbol of spirit and matter, descending to the earth, striking root, and then re-ascending heavenward again. The triple-leaved palâsa is a symbol of the triple essence in the Universe—Spirit, Soul, Matter. The dark cypress was the world-tree of Mexico, and is now with the Christians and Mahomedans the emblem of death, of peace and rest. The fir was held sacred in Egypt, and its cone was carried in religious processions, though now it has almost disappeared from the land of the mummies; so also was the sycamore, the tamarisk, the palm and the vine. The sycamore was the Tree of Life in Egypt, and also in Assyria. It was sacred to Hathor at Heliopolis; and is now sacred in the same place to the Virgin Mary. Its juice was precious by virtue of its occult powers, as the Soma is with Brahmans, and Haoma with the Parsis. "The fruit and sap of the Tree of Life bestow immortality." A large volume might be written upon these sacred trees of antiquity, the reverence for some of which has survived to this day, without exhausting the subject.
—H. P. Blavatsky, *The Theosophical Glossary*

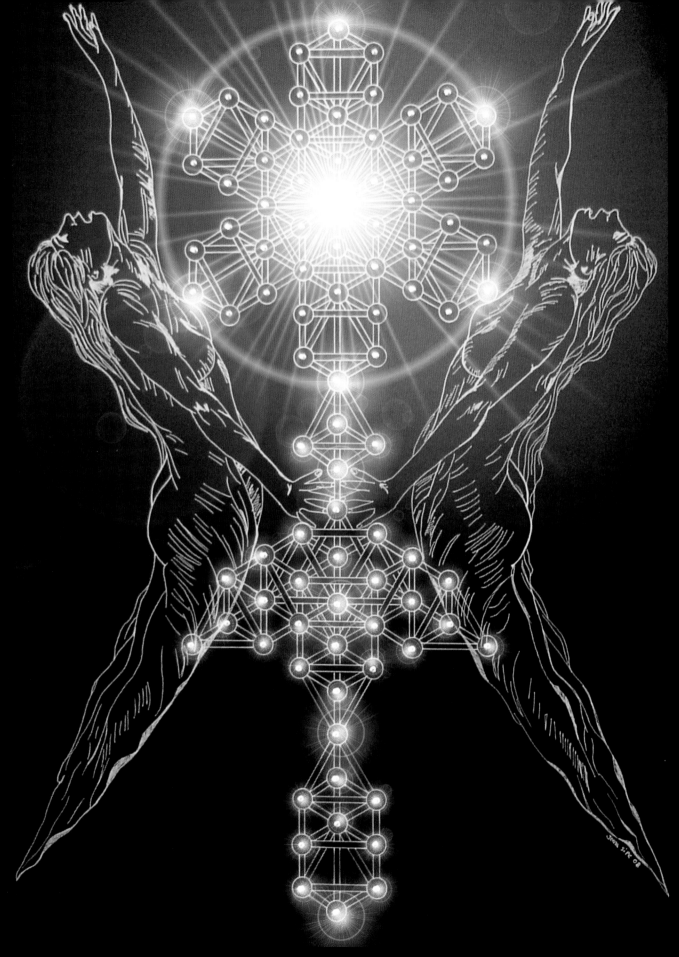

I AM TIRED OF TEARS *(Panel in silver and gold ink and crystals on black card, 70 x 50 cm, 2008)*

ANGELS HANDS *(Panel in silver and gold ink and crystals on black card, 70 x 50 cm, 2008)*

THE DAWN SADNESS *(Panel in silver and gold ink and crystals on black card, 70 x 50 cm, 2008)*

I AM

At that ball on fire that is my burning heart,
I put on my belly the whole hope
Of the world and gave birth
To the universal creation.
For within me I made the bread
For all mankind, and my blood
Has become the leaven that leavened it.
I am all life; I am all creation.
The oven that bakes the bread of the world,
I am.
The dragonfly pond and the lake fish.
The One who always has been.
The One who is. The One who will be.
I am.
The light of humanity, I am.
The Infant unborn.
He who waits for the whisper of the future,
In the womb of nature,
Flying south with the birds.

I AM TIRED OF TEARS

Tears.
Tears.
Tears.
And more tears.
I'm sick of tears.

ANGELS' HANDS

Erase forever the fireball which you have cast
 Into my heart.
The hands of the Angels who came, when I begged help,
Were brightening in red and orange,
Showing the flickering light that also existed in my heart.
The Inexhaustible Fountain was now destroyed.
The skies had become dark,
And I was crowned with thorns.
My throat was burning and was burning inside.
My guts died and my voice cracked
And I could not speak.
The ultimate end had arrived,
And all the lights of the earth had gone,
Until finally the Black Angel fell on my body
And ended the crystalline silver cord
That has always joined me to life.
And I let myself go and become united
With the oceans and tides and water in drops of dew,
And current in the rivers and wind in the mountains
And vastness of blue skies.
And I died.
My body has died, and my little spark of light
Merged with the universe, and I became One.

THE DAWN SADNESS

How I do feel like contemplating
Only eternity
And a day of spring
In that one when the flowers
Keep on blooming
And the grief of the morning
Ends with the darkness of the night.

Sacred Lines and Poetry

These are all works that I have done using sacred geometry and mandalas energetically condensing the Light of the cosmos and the universe. There are so many different forms of using geometry as it appears all around us. Inside nature, inside a petal or a flower there are so many geometrical shapes; inside a star from the sea we can realize how the Creator intended to use geometrical forms to produce harmony and balance in the universal order.

The forms advance from very simple ones— such as the rectangle, the circle, the triangle—to more elaborate ones that connect the energetic properties of the primary forms to create new forms. These more elaborate forms give to those who can see beyond matter a new perspective about the real Essence behind all matter and all that we see with our physical eyes.

The poetry is created to the form and vice-versa; many times the form is created first, and then the poetry comes slowly to form the equilibrium that is intended for the message of the painting.

Almost every time that I am painting, I use calm music to establish a sacred and profound environment around myself in which the patterns and all the right forms emerge. This is like an atmosphere of ethereal shadows that absorbs my entire being completely, providing the energy that I need in order to paint using the gold and silver pens and then to establish the correct places for the crystals, "illuminate" the painting with color effects, and, finally, permit the words of poetry to flow like a drop of water in a calm lake.

The lines that make up well-known shapes such as rectangles, squares, triangles, or circles are energetic forms of condensed light that I draw with a specific objective. Nothing is created by accident, and no line is drawn that does not belong to that part of the painting. When I have an inner feeling that nothing more is needed, the process stops suddenly and no more lines can be drawn on that particular painting. This way I know that the creative process has come to an end and that it is time to receive the necessary indications about where to locate the crystals. I go through almost the same process as well with the "illumination" of the works with color.

Regarding poetry, I can say that I love to write. My first book with fifty-four poems

called *I Drowned Myself in You* was written in 2005. In it I talk about my connection with the sea—especially the stormy and cloudy days in addition to an angry sea, the dark gray clouds, and rain, thunder, and cold afternoons when the sun is going down and the night is coming to take its place. The second poetry book, *Behind the Tombstones*, published a year after the first one, basically concerns the same nature themes but relates them to feelings of love. It is a sentimental book and a very intimate one, speaking of personal emotions and ways of thinking in a poetical language. Last year was published *Echoes of Silence*, which has a total of 136 poems and which I consider to be my major poetical work so far.

I speak through my poems especially of love, not only the human-to-human love but also unconditional love, the love that has no boundaries or preconception of any kind.

And I love to make poetry about the forces of nature that I compare to the inner forces of the human being. The natural powers of rain, sun, mist, shadows, thunder, sea, wind, and so, so many others I often compare to human feelings of love, anger, sadness, joy, and enlightenment. For me, the energy is totally the same, and the poems speak about that.

I also blend mystical and occult themes among the words of nature and feelings. So the poem is transformed into a complete treatise of representing by words the Inner Human Essence that inhabits each human being as his or her own and true reality.

Requiem aeternam dona ei, Domine, et lux perpetua luceat ei.
Te decet hymnus, Deus, in Sion, et tibi reddetur votum in Jerusalem:
Exaudi orationem meam, ad te omnis caro veniet.
Requiem aeternam dona ei, Domine,
Et lux perpetua luceat ei.

Grant them eternal rest, O Lord, and let perpetual light shine upon them.
A hymn becomes you, O God, in Zion, and to you shall a vow be repaid
In Jerusalem.
Hear my prayer; to you shall all flesh come.
Eternal rest grant unto them, O Lord,
And let perpetual light shine upon them.

from "The Requiem Mass" (*Missa pro defunctis*)

***LUX PERPETUA* (ETERNAL LIGHT)** *(Panel in silver ink and crystals on black canvas, 90 x 70 cm, 2008)*

WILD BLOOD *(Panel in silver ink and crystals on black paper, 80 x 60 cm, 2008)*

THE KEY OF LIFE *(Panel in silver pen and crystals on black canvas, 120 x 90 cm, 2006)*

THE KEY OF LIFE

With the Key of Life that reaches all and opens both sides,
In a Universe without fear, where inner Peace exists,
I am afraid of nothing, and in the veil of time the past exists
No more.
All came from far,
In the boats of Light that I have made for myself.
I receive in my arms and make necklaces of petals
With the autumn roses.
I receive worship of prayers and incense from the highest.
Crowns are dressed in carmine, the color of my eternal eyes.
Tender are the lights that shine in my sight.

LUX PERPETUA (ETERNAL LIGHT)

There is the lightness of my being and the lightness of my body,
The light of my spirit, and the serenity of my soul.
When the two come together in a calm sea,
No more tears appear in my face.
My greatest wish would be that this light could be eternal
Inside of me.

WILD BLOOD

One intense Light dressed with my feelings.
I wake up now. It is still night.
The dawn will not come so soon.
Come. Delight yourself again.
Dawn knows the violence inside me.
And inside,
Wild is my blood.
Crystalline and hidden,
In the cavities of my Being.

(Panel in silver and gold ink and crystals on black canvas, 70 x 70 cm, 2006)

ANIMA FLAMMA (THE FLAME OF THE SOUL)

In the obscure exhaustiveness of dawns, no more Beings of Light are born.

There are no more Buddhas on the sacred river's shores.

There are no more Nirvanas to achieve that can melt down

My most intense desires.

Now that the tides have calmed down and the rivers to the seas return,

Now that the beggars ask for Light on the edges of the ways,

Now that the mists flood my eyes,

It is not I who talks but the One that speaks through me to the world.

THE CODE OF THE SOUL *(Panel in silver and gold ink and crystals on black card, 70 x 50 cm, 2008)*

COME FROM FAR AWAY *(Panel in silver and gold ink and crystals on black card, 70 x 50 cm, 2008)*

THE CLIFFS BETWEEN US *(Panel in gold ink and crystals on black card, 70 x 50 cm, 2008)*

THE CODE OF THE SOUL

You that came from the stars within the
Galaxies of Infinite Spaces, discover, in yourself,
The eternal beauty of the worlds that populate
The abysmal, infinite, black Space.
I gave you a code so that you can decipher
Your soul.
Read and remember
All that you had forgotten,
But that remains in you.
Read and remember.
Discover the past that becomes present
In every remembrance of thyself.

COME FROM FAR AWAY

I do not want more eternal days.
I wanted to learn in love
The Light of being peaceful.
The war inside consumes me
Every time I start the journey.
I despair for not being able to know.
I slap, mourning, in fury against the
Bitter voice that gives me no rest.
I embrace, once again, all the pain
Of the parting.
Stay a little more. Let me remind you.
The coffee is cooled now
And the fire burns no more.
The night is cold and in the blankets
You I no longer encounter.
Come. Come from afar.
Come spend one more night with me.
So that in the meeting of tears
Once again I see you and
Wish you to go back again to miss you more.

SILVER MIRACLES

I am surrounded by angels on the cliff
Where I am.
Angels of light that softly embrace me.
I feel the peace that inhabits
On the windy cliffs of the mountain of my soul.
Made of Light are the Miracles that I produce
And of silver the dimension from where they are born.

THE CLIFFS BETWEEN US

I would not like to see you go. Do not go today.
Wait for the heavenly car that will deliver you to the heavens.
In tiredness of waiting I wait in me by the starlight.
There is a time that passes and does not return.
The waters move within me, within my blood.
I absorb in despair the air that you have already breathed
And do not regret of being myself.
The One who declares himself to the world and expects
Nothing from it.
I've opened the doors to the storms and picked rosemary
On the slopes behind the house.
On the thunderstorms in the clear nights mature by the rain,
I rest myself in you and watch the days go by.
Without clouds to promise me anything.
Not knowing or being what you want me to be.
I let myself be this way. Abandoned. Begging out of hunger,
Hunger for a feeling from you.
For a look that could make everything pass away.
For a hug that will give warmth to my skin.
I am shaded.
I intoxicated myself with the feeling and fell, forgotten,
In the night,
Among the cliffs between us that we could not overcome.

VENI CREATOR SPIRITUS
(COME, HOLY SPIRIT)

Veni Creator Spiritus,
Mentes tuorum visita,
Imple superna gratia,
Quae tu creasti pectora.

Come Holy Spirit, Creator, come
From your bright heavenly throne,
Come take possession of our souls
And make them all your own.

(Panel in silver and gold ink and crystals
on black card, 70 x 50 cm, 2008)

I looked into the uncertain for the final moment of liberation.

I have lived many lives,

But this is the one in which I lose myself and search.

In the empty spaces of my soul,

I am an obscure reason to live another day.

From permanent broken pieces am I made,

From rock walls dreamed through which I hear the sounds of whispering green.

A long time ago I forgot the white riots, ignited

The flames of the highest mountains.

And now, I remain obscure no more.

The Light comes upon me and does not recede.

Love hidden in me comes forth and does not recede.

I am the One,

The immortal God of the heavens of your soul,

The One who intoxicates himself with the nectar of the heavens

And never dies. The body can disappear with the rotted land,

But the soul will never become intoxicated with it.

From the Lotus in the heart, A flower

LAMENT *(Panel in silver and gold ink and crystals on black card, 70 x 50 cm, 2008)*

COR FLAMMIS (HEART´S FLAME) *(Panel in gold and silver ink and crystals on black canvas, 90 x 70 cm, 2008)*

A DROP FROM MY BLOOD AND THE SPRING FLOWERS *(Panel in silver ink and crystals on black paper, 70 x 50 cm, 2009)*

INVOCATION *(Panel in silver ink and crystals on black paper, 7 0 x 50 cm, 2009)*

GUARDIANS OF THE SPIRIT *(Panel in silver ink and crystals on black paper, 70 x 50 cm, 2009)*

MOMENTS *(Panel in silver and gold ink and crystals on black paper, 80 x 60 cm, 2009)*

LAMENT

Listen to my regret. Dream.
Hear my voice. Wake up.
Inebriate my spirit with thy Light.
Reveal to me the burning flame
Of my heart.
Dream. Wake up. Live. Die.
Be born.
Live the Moment that never returns.
Be one with the eternal Now.
Share the peace that exists in the
Open immensities of your Body.

COR FLAMMIS (HEART´S FLAME)

Today the world is inebriated with the smells of my Soul.
I destroy the powers of heaven to meet in me the missed snows
Of the sudden sunshine that no longer exists.
I reach God just to ask him for one more second,
One second when I will be at your side, lost to the world.
The boats return to the black shore
And I whisper for the winds that are gone.
Give me the silent mists, full of incense to hide my wild spirit.
Give me dawns full of inert looks
And left out by the rain of the past.
Give me love. Give me love.
For there is only love that I need in me. . . .

A DROP FROM MY BLOOD AND THE SPRING FLOWERS

I seek Thee at the top of the ice ridges,
Yearning to know.
I seek Thee in the hidden cliffs of the unknown,
Where the nights still frighten me
And the darkness has left me.
I look for Thee to give me to you,
To receive Thy remembrance
And nestle me in Thy lap, asking for protection.
I seek Thee to receive love,
To give what you gave me,
To get what you have to give to me.
Looking for you in the vastness of the forest,
Knowing that I'll meet you.
Express Yourself in me. Be one with my body.
Inebriate Thyself with my perfume.
I have to give Thee a drop from my blood and the spring flowers.

INVOCATION

De profundis clamavi ad te, Domine;
Domine, exaudi vocem meam. Fiant aures tuae intendentes
In vocem deprecationis meae.
Si iniquitates observaveris, Domine, Domine, quis sustinebit?
Quia apud te propitiatio est; et propter legem tuam sustinui te, Domine.
Sustinuit anima mea in verbo ejus: Speravit anima mea in Domino.

From the depths, I have cried out to you, O Lord;
Lord, hear my voice. Let your ears be attentive
To the voice of my supplication.
If you, Lord, were to mark iniquities, who, O Lord, shall stand?
For with you is forgiveness; and because of your law, I stood by you, Lord.
My soul has stood by his word. My soul has hoped in the Lord.

—from Psalm 130

GUARDIANS OF THE SPIRIT

I pretend not to see.
I love what I cannot.
Nothing is impossible for the soul
That wanders.
Alone. In the world alone. With springs
of clear and pure waters in my eyes.
Alone. By the immensity of dense fog.
Alone. Keeping the Spirit.
Guarding the One who never dies.
Alone. With the Soul open to the world.
Inside the Spirit without time or space.
Without snow falling.
Without waters that balance.
Inside the timeless,
Transcendental magic of my Being.

MOMENTS

Days pass slowly by me.
Slowly, with no rush, no fear,
I take the stick, as the cloak
And the shroud I carry
Through the wet floor.
There are moments that never come back;
These are the ones that have died.
There are moments that will never die;
These are the ones that always return.

THE ONES WHO KNOW THEMSELVES *(Panel in silver ink and crystals on black paper, 70 x 50 cm, 2009)*

THE ONES WHO HAD BORN TWICE *(Panel in silver ink and crystals on black paper, 70 x 50 cm, 2009)*

MANY MOONS *(Panel in silver ink and crystals on black paper, 70 x 50 cm, 2009)*

WHERE THE ANGELS ARE BORN *(Panel in silver ink and crystals on black paper, 80 x 60 cm, 2009)*

THE LAST SECRET *(Panel in silver and gold ink and crystals on black paper, 80 x 60 cm, 2009)*

THE ONES WHO KNOW THEMSELVES

I am special, a winged angel in a world of
Beings without wings.
I am special, a morning fog that comes off
The coast and looks forward to reaching the sea.
I am special, I am that laugh
That makes you believe, that gives you hope
In beautiful days of wonders.
I am special. The one that bathes your body
With massages, using sweet oils.
I know myself. I know who I am.
Neither more centuries, nor the lives
Of past reincarnations defeat me.
I know myself. I know your innermost being.
I know who you are. But you do not know me.
Come to me. I will give thee the nectar
Of self-knowledge that will make you free.

THE ONES WHO HAD BORN TWICE

I was born in this body,
But there have been so many births
That I have lost count.
I will no longer be a cocoon
To become again a dragonfly.
I will be no more a drop in the ocean,
Dragged into the vastness of the wind.
I no longer fear death.
I am the Twice Born,
The Immortal of the Mongolian steppes.
The One who is part of the sacred Wall
Of the Guardians of the Flame.
I am the intense heat and the harsh cold,
The pure silk thread that unites mankind.
I am the beauty of the human eye,
The blood flowing in your body and mine.
The Energy in Human Light; what is
Born to die, what dies to be born again.

MANY MOONS

The twilight burns inside of me.
The light that I embrace agonizes me.
The moon loves me.
She kisses my hidden face,
That brings me forgotten memories.

WHERE THE ANGELS ARE BORN

I am the One from the Virgin Forests
Of the Abysses. . . .
Recognize yourself in me,
Winged Dragon of a Thousand Stars.
I am born in the warm embers
Of the stormy seas,
I come to shore from time to time,
When searching for my light
That disappeared in the twilight.
I satisfy your hunger, if you let me.
I feed you with my light, if you possess me.
Where can you be that I am not?
Where can I be that you are not?
I am an ally of the eagles in the mountains,
Unbreakable wall of the immensity of the night.
I am a hawk and a winged hummingbird.
I was born there. I also will die there—
There, in the holy place, in the Hidden Home,
Where the Angels are born.

THE LAST SECRET

No more secrets are hidden in the arcs of time,
What flourished in the fields soaked by the rains
In May has rotted,
And me, with these flowers, became dead to myself;
I'm a new depository where new wine can be poured.
I am the last secret,
The one who opens the Ark of the Covenant.

WHITE SOUL

White Soul, pure, appalled by time;
White soul, washed by the patina of thought;
White soul, obscured by the passing cloud.
Feline animal, bird of prey flying.
White soul, blackened by the foliage of mist,
Intense in perfume, collected on drops of desire,
Fragrances in horizons that are lost,
Vacant stares, in crystallized mansions.
White soul, enveloped by the patina of thought,
Adrift in the intensity of the wave that arrives.
They smile to me at the cafes, the souls that wander,
Lost in the streets. Absorbed in thought,
They do not love; they lie when they love;
They get dirty in the mud of feigned emotion.
Dress me in a robe, purified in rosemary,
White as the purple of the cotton that eludes me,
On the opium where I fulfill my appetites, my pleasures,
Where I fulfill the need for purity in me.

*(Panel in silver and gold ink and crystals on
black canvas, 90 x 70 cm, 2010)*

The Cathedrals of the Soul

The Cathedrals of the Soul are buildings of Light and Energy within the Human Being. They are the hidden and symbolic representation of our inner journey and our discovery of the Divinity within.

They represent the Brightness of the ethereal, alchemical heart of the Shape that appears in successive incarnations and that never becomes extinguished or evolves.

The Shape is She herself, through endless time and endless ages.

In the Cathedral paintings, I tried to represent the stages of the human soul, combining them in nine different phases of life. When I reached the ninth Cathedral, I no longer had any inspiration, so I stopped there and made no more. The process of evolution was finished. I called this last one "The Return" and so originally thought that the first one should be called "Birth." But then I realized that instead I needed to call the first one "Before Birth," representing the stage between lives and before the Soul has chosen a particular body in which to reincarnate. So the first Cathedral is about the phase of that choosing and considering all the odds. Then "Birth" and "After Birth" follow as stages two and three.

"Childhood" is the name I have chosen for the fourth stage, both for the Soul and for the human form that is its vehicle for incarnation. The fifth stage is related to the fourth, and this Cathedral represents "Learning." I understand this stage as a stage of remembering what has been forgotten from past lives and needs now in the present life to be brought forth again.

Besides the knowledge that is common and is simply remembered, there is another kind of knowledge that the human form is asked to give to his or her own Soul. This kind of knowledge is represented in the next three Cathedrals and is related to Love; hence their names "To Love," "To be Loved," and "To Love and to be Loved." Most of us spend our entire lives only loving and others only in being loved; there are so few of us who are able to experience both. I consider it a blessing to have this feeling and to share it with other people.

The last Cathedral, as I have mentioned, is called "The Return," meaning the return to the Father, to the Primordial Essence from which comes every Soul and every human form. In this Cathedral, we have all come back Home.

THE CATHEDRALS OF THE SOUL SERIES *(Panels in silver ink and crystals on black paper, 60 x 80cm, 2010)*

THE RETURN

The Portals of the Spirit

The Portals of the Spirit are entrances for the meditation of the Soul, portals that are open to the most sensitive. They evolve from the more complex physical body, or dense matter, to the simplest one: the Universal Spirit that penetrates and dwells in everything, as Light or so-called Love.

The Portals are simple structures, but they form designs that reach my inner senses with light and energy, inducing balance between my emotions and my thoughts. They permit me to go beyond the mortal body and reach the place from where everything emanates and is created.

I created seven Portals, because seven is the number of order inside creation and because,

as has happened with all the other series, no inspiration arrived when I tried to create the next one.

So these Portals represent the different stages of the Essence, starting in the *Sthula Sharira*, the human body, and progressing to the *Linga Sharira*, the ethereal double, and then to the *Prâna*, representing the vital energy that sustains the human body.

The fourth one, *Kama Rupa*, is the astral body, followed by the *Manas*, the mental body.

The final two are the "higher" representation of the Essence; they are the *Buddhi*, or the Spiritual Soul, and the *Atman*, representing the Monad or the Divine Essence.

THE PORTALS OF THE SPIRIT SERIES
(Panels in silver ink on black paper, 60 x 80cm, 2009)

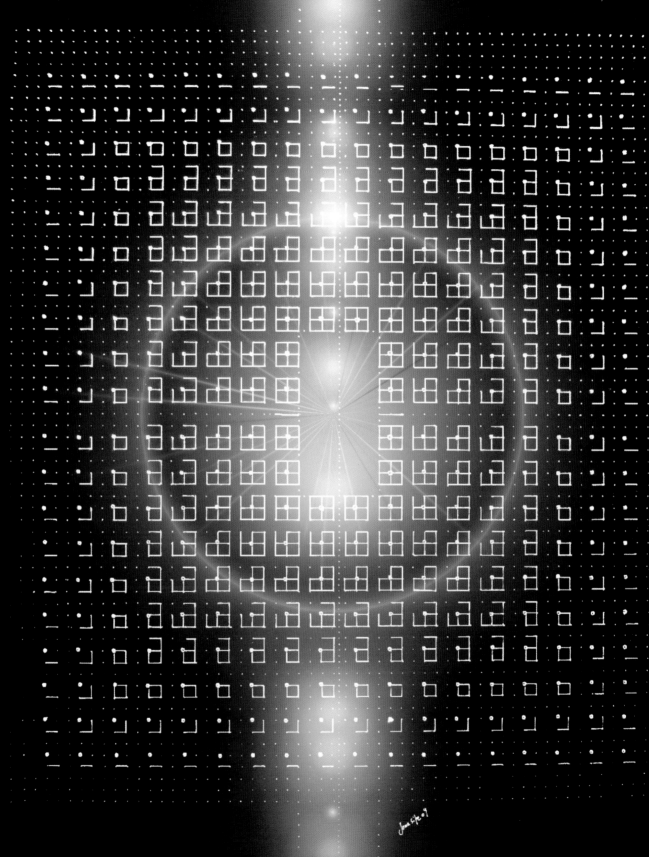

PORTAL OF THE SPIRIT 1: *STHULA SHARIRA*

Annamaya kosha is equivalent to *Sthula Sharira*, meaning the gross body, physical or material. It is the
first "shell" of the Monad of the five given by the Vedas, which is known by the name of *principle*.

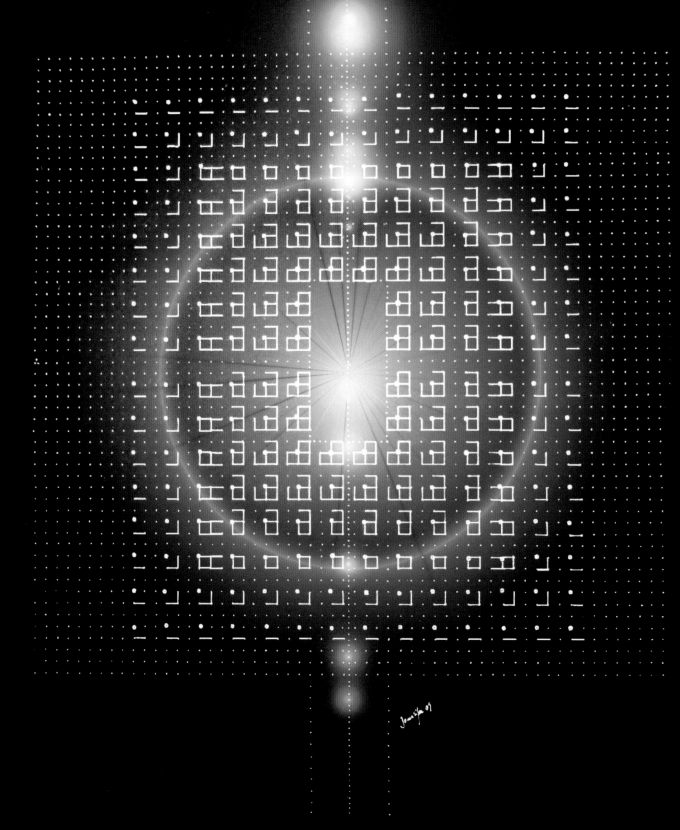

PORTAL OF THE SPIRIT 2: *LINGA SHARIRA*

Linga Sharira is derived from *linga*, meaning "model," and *sharira*, which comes from
the verbal root *sri*, meaning "double." It designates the second principle in the septenary
constitution of humankind, which is slightly more ethereal than the physical body (*Sthula Sharira*).
It permeates the entire human body, being a cast of all organs, arteries, and nerves.

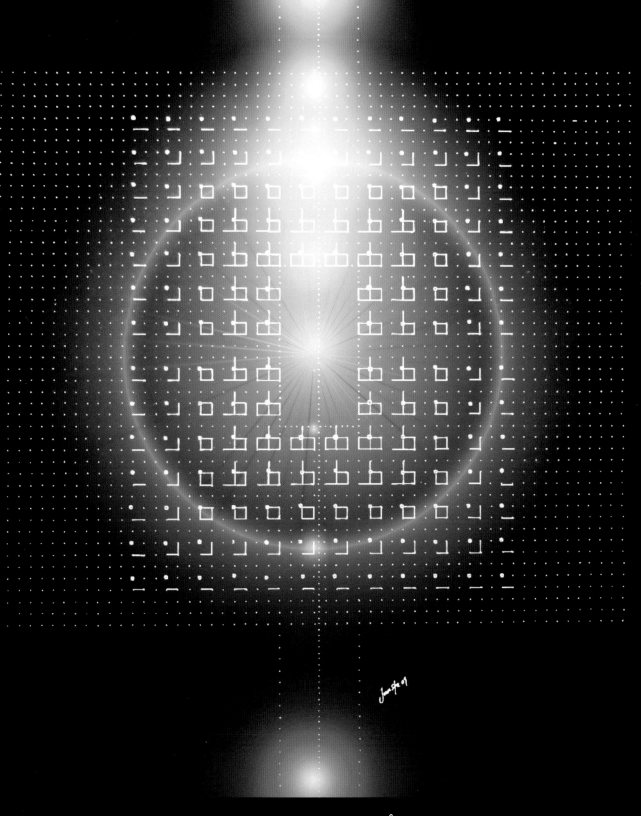

PORTAL OF THE SPIRIT 3: *PRÂNA*

Prâna or *pranan* in Sanskrit is derived from *pra*, or "before," plus the verbal root *an*,
meaning "to breathe" or "to live." It designates the third principle in the septenary constitution
of man. *Prâna* is the vital psychic energy that keeps the physical body functioning.

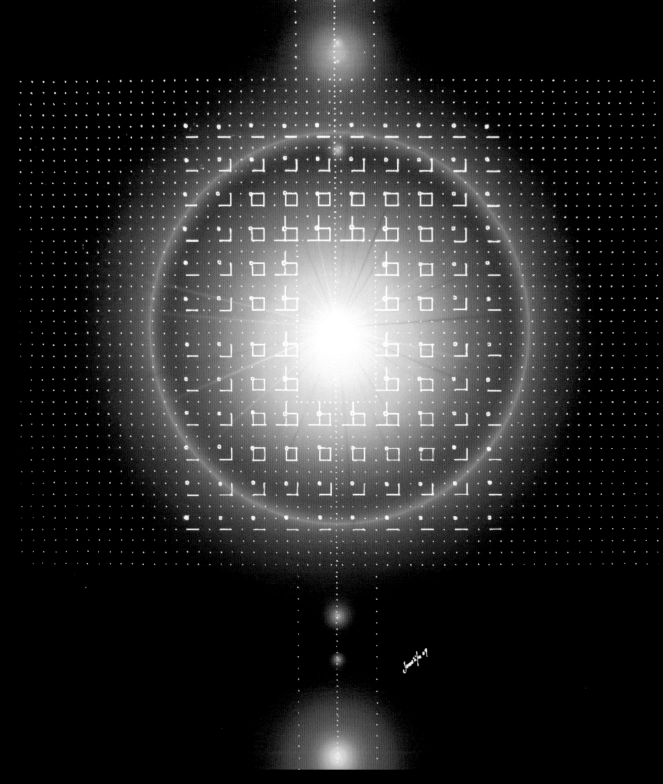

PORTAL OF THE SPIRIT 4: *KĀMA RUPA*

Kāma Rupa (in Sanskrit: *kāma*, "desire"; *rupa*, "form") is also known as the "desire body," the "emotional body," or the "astral body." It denotes the fourth principle in the septenary constitution of man.

PORTAL OF THE SPIRIT 5: *MANAS*

Manas (from the Sanskrit root for "man" or "think") is a reflection of the fifth principle
in the septenary constitution of man, and its nature is dual. *Manas* in higher essence
(higher *manas*) is the "thinker" in us, our true and divine mind. The inferior *manas* is defined
as the mental body, which tends to ally itself with desire (*kama*). *Manas* has the task of
uniting the animal part to the spiritual part of the human being.

PORTAL OF THE SPIRIT 6: *BUDDHI*

Buddhi (from the Sanskrit verbal root, *budh*, "awaken," "enlighten," "to know") is the sixth
principle in the septenary constitution of man. It is the spiritual soul, the thin vessel in which burns
the *Atman*, the Spirit. It is the single ray that emanates from the universal Soul. Along with the
Atman and *Manas*, *buddhi* forms the higher Triad—the incorruptible and immortal part.

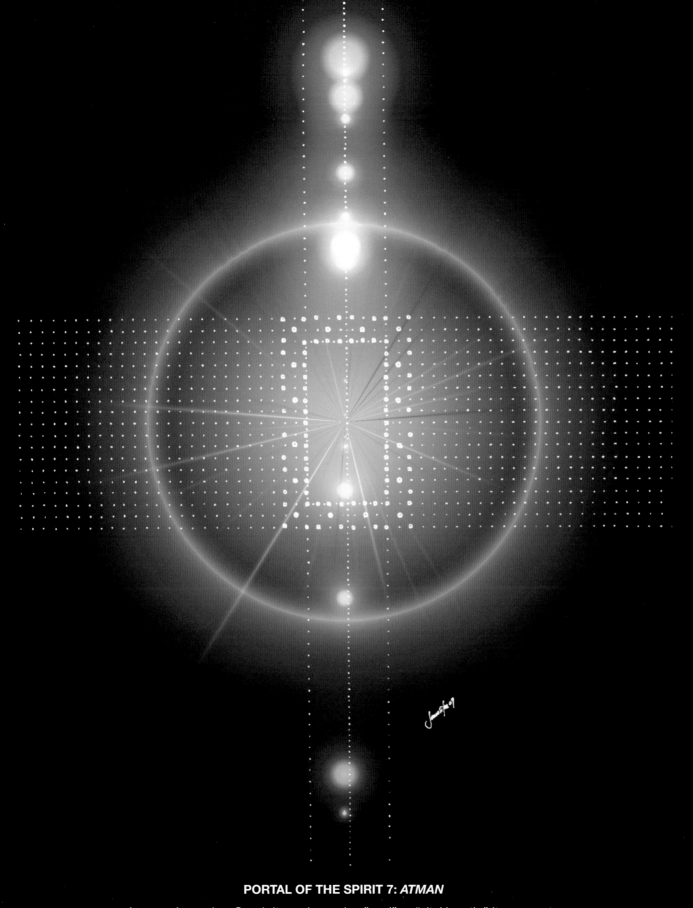

PORTAL OF THE SPIRIT 7: *ATMAN*

Atma or *Atman* is a Sanskrit word meaning "soul" or "vital breath." It represents
the *Monad*, the highest principle of the human being. The *Atman* is the abstract idea of "myself."
It is the highest human principle, the essence of God, indivisible and formless.

Inspired Messages

The following series of messages were written and designed to be offered as a gift in 2009 at Christmas to some close friends. As the sacred geometry of the mandalas came to form, simultaneously the poetry was written for them. It was not an ordinary process, as has been true with many other ones.

In this case, the messages were "coming" to me along with the lines, circles, points, and crystals of the paintings. They were coming so rapidly to my mind and hands that, in fact, I think that I only spent—if we could count the hours—only a single day to do all six and to finish the poetry texts for each. This can be an entirely exhausting process of creation.

The original people for whom the paintings were intended received them. Only later were the paintings "illuminated" with colors, as they appear in this version. Five of them were used in the 2010 winter issue of *Quest*, the magazine of the Theosophical Society in America.

THE MESSAGE SERIES
(Panels in silver and gold ink and crystals on black paper, 70 x 50cm, 2009)

MESSAGE 1

MESSAGE 2

MESSAGE 3

MESSAGE 4

MESSAGE 5

MESSAGE 6

MESSAGE 1

Fixed stars in a hidden universe,
Within thee and thy being.
Lights that are discovered in the heart of
The living light,
In your body and your look.
There is a universe of galaxies in thee,
That surrounds the verdant valleys.
There is a Shepherd who loves you,
And, hidden, veils you,
A certainty that your soul is eternal.

MESSAGE 2

Twilights of pain that fade away.
Only the physical suffers; remind yourself
Of your immortality.
The consolation of heavens is within your heart,
Thy treasure beats in unison with it.
The hidden foliage and the veils of
Time dissipate,
So that you may contemplate thyself.
Son of the most High and Being without
Fleeting lives,
Your Father is your inexhaustible source
Of eternal life.

MESSAGE 3

Do not worry about what doesn´t come,
With what you know to be light as the breeze.
May you reach the high thought of the
Heavenly spheres.
You will see in you the light of seven candles lit.
If you look inside your heart,
You will be one with all and with the magical universe.
Today, just today, live the opportunity that was
Given thee,
To be Love, from the early centuries.

MESSAGE 4

Share yourself, review the dreams that you lived today;
Remember yourself, remember who you are.
There's a light in you that will never be extinguished,
A lit candle, made of an immortal wax.
Take away the velvet veil that shrouds your eyes
And see.
With the bobcats look at thy own beauty and light.
The shadows will be nothing
Before the hidden tranquility of your serene heart.

MESSAGE 5

Your lives do not matter anymore,
Neither what you were nor what you will be.
It only matters what you are now,
The moment you have now is given to you at all times.
There are memories in you, memories that you
Did not forget,
Many lives have passed, but this is the only one
In which you are alive.
Be who you are, a light torch and an awakened heart,
An illuminated Force inside and all around you.

MESSAGE 6

I know who you are and the love that
Lives there in your open heart.
I know of the sharing that you have
To give so you can receive.
There is a secret hidden
From the bygone days,
That is to be yourself,
Truthful to your still heart.
Everything that is secret
Is of your knowledge.
Love thyself; give the gift
That is also given to you.
Love everyone who comes to you
In search of love,
Because only love is what you are
And only love can you share.

Quest Books

encourages open-minded inquiry into
world religions, philosophy, science, and the arts
in order to understand the wisdom of the ages,
respect the unity of all life, and help people explore
individual spiritual self-transformation.

Its publications are generously supported by
The Kern Foundation,
a trust committed to Theosophical education.

Quest Books is the imprint of
the Theosophical Publishing House,
a division of the Theosophical Society in America.
For information about programs, literature,
on-line study, membership benefits, and international centers,
see www.theosophical.org
or call 800-669-1571 or (outside the US) 630-668-1571.

Related Quest Titles

The Chakras, by C. W. Leadbeater

Isis Unveiled, by H. P. Blavatsky

Mandala: Luminous Symbols for Healing,
by Judith Cornell

*The One True Adventure: Theosophy and the
Quest for Meaning*, by Joy Mills

The Personal Aura, by Dora van Gelder Kunz

The Secret Doctrine, by H. P. Blavatsky

The Voice of the Silence, by H. P. Blavatsky

To order books or a complete Quest catalog,
call 800-669-9425 or (outside the US) 630-665-0130.

Praise for Joma Sipe's
Soul of Light

"My guess is that these works will resonate with the reader's very core of being as they do with mine—which is where the real power in this book lies."

—from the foreword by Thomas Ockerse,
award-winning designer and Professor of Graphic Design,
Rhode Island School of Design

"Sipe gives visual form to the energetic patterns contained in a vast array of spiritual texts and traditions. He generously shares his process of creating these remarkable images that seem channeled through his inner being, enabling the viewer to intuit how each spiritual path is both unique and at its root connected to one infinite Source. This important book instructs us in a way that transcends dogma and touches the universal spark within us all."

—Pat B. Allen, artist and author of
Art Is a Way of Knowing and *Art Is a Spiritual Path*

"*Soul of Light* reverently presents the multidimensional depths of our universe. A timeless treasure with which to vision and dream."

—Ruth A. Drayer, author of *Nicholas & Helena Roerich:
The Spiritual Journey of Two Great Artists and Peacemakers*